DON'T REWRITE THE BOOK

WRITTEN BY

QUINCINA C. DAVIS

Published By: TamikaINK

Library of Congress Cataloging-in-Publication Data has been applied for

ISBN: 9798852906458

PRINTED IN THE UNITED STATES OF AMERICA

Dedication

I dedicate this book to my wonderful, loving children, Quintequa and Jarvis Jr. You are my inspiration for writing this book. I appreciate you so much and I love you dearly.

Your mom, Quin

Table of Contents

Introduction

Everyone has a unique story. Some have a similar experience but no experience is exactly alike. Why? Because we come from different paths of life. We all have fingerprints and none of them are exactly the same. Even twin fingerprints are not exactly the same. They have similar features but not the same fingerprints. In this world, there are many counterfeits. This is why we must know what is authentic and what is counterfeit. There is no replica or cloning of God's design. We are unique and God has designed it this way because He wants to get the glory out of our lives. Every story has a theme, plot, setting, character, point of view, conflict, and resolution. Every now and then there may be a plot twist. Each of our stories are composed of all of these elements. We may experience some unexpected situations along the way but we must understand that there is nothing that catches God by surprise. He is omniscient. He knows everything.

You have a story and I have a story. Our stories were written by the finger of Almighty God our Creator. God had us in His infinite mind from the beginning of time. He has already written our story and all we have to do is follow the path that He has chosen for us since the beginning of time. We must follow the directions and instructions which He has given us and not reroute the path. We get in trouble when we deter from the original path God has designated and ordained for us to follow.

If we make the decision to reroute our steps it causes chaos and destruction. We should never think that we have the authority or power to rewrite our story or our own finite version of it. Your story is exciting and will always be exciting! Your story is infused with wonder, excitement, beauty, inspiration, drama, suspense, humor, and more. Your story is unique, fascinating, and compelling. It needs to be heard, proclaimed, and embraced. God the Creator of Heaven and Earth has written and signed our story with His signet of love. Life is not always a bed of roses. We will encounter some tough and difficult times along the way but we have to trust in the Lord with all our heart and lean not unto our own understanding. In all our ways acknowledge Him, and He shall direct our paths (Proverbs 3:5, 6). Dearly beloved, whatever you may have to face on this path called life, "Don't Rewrite the Book, Embrace Your Story!"

CHAPTER 1
A Reality Check

L ife has a way of revealing reality. Many of us are living in a fantasy land unknowingly. I thought that I was all right just the way I was but in all reality, it was a lie. The enemy of our soul has a way of deceiving us into thinking that all is well and life is full of peaches and cream but what he will not reveal to us is that he is lying to us and setting us up to be destroyed. I was not saved, sanctified, and filled with the Holy Spirit. I did not have Jesus in my life and God Almighty on my side. The enemy (devil) knows how to paint an extraordinary, beautiful, irresistible picture that he wants us to see, but it is only a mirage. A mirage is an optical illusion, something that you believe you see but really isn't there. An example of a mirage is when you believe that you see water on the highway while driving. If you notice, while you are driving it looks and appears to be water but when you reach the destination you realize that it is only the highway and there is no water at all. The enemy wants you and I to believe his lies. The enemy is the originator of lies (John 8:44).

In November of 1999, I had an encounter with God. I woke up one morning from a night of partying. When I awakened, the conviction of the Holy Spirit was my portion and I felt so bad. It was as if I had committed the unthinkable. I do not know how the Lord dealt with others but as for me, I was under conviction for a long time. I was raised in a Baptist church and I heard about how Jesus was crucified and died on the cross for my sin but I did not understand all of it. Even though I had heard of Him, I never accepted Him as my Lord and Savior. As I began to get up, I started crying. It felt as if the weight of the world was on my shoulders. I kneeled before the Lord because I was taught at a young age that God was real.

I told God, "I have done wrong and Lord I do not know how to get saved. Lord, I don't even know how to repent but if you save me I will live for you all the days of my life." As I kneeled and cried out to the Lord, I felt the burdens and the weight of the world lifting off my shoulders and I felt like running!

While the presence of the Lord was still with me, God Almighty gave me instructions to leave the place where I was living, not only the city but the whole entire state. I am reminded of what God spoke to Abraham. God told Abraham to leave the country, get from around his family, and He would show him where to go (Genesis 12:1).

After I calmed down from weeping and mourning, I started preparing myself for change. The first thing the Lord instructed me to do was to leave my hometown. I packed my clothes and headed down Interstate 95. Once I crossed the N.C. state line, I felt a burden lift off my shoulders. I felt free! For the record, my hometown was not the issue, it was the Lord's way of getting me where He had destined for me to be. God knows the plans He has for us (Jeremiah 29:11).

When I crossed the state line and saw the N.C. sign, I knew from that moment that everything about my life was getting ready to change and that this was a new beginning for me. I knew within myself that the Lord was about to make all things new concerning me.

God will bring us to a place in Him where the eyes of the soul will come open and He will reveal to us where we are really headed. Many times we have the faintest idea about where we are, where we are going, and who we really are. I was headed down the wrong path and at a point of no return but God Almighty, the one who sits high and looks low, who knows all things, reached down to pull my wretched, unrested soul out of the snare of the devil.

God is the only one who can deliver us from the snares, tricks, devices, and strategies of the devil that desires to hold us captive and in bondage. We must allow God to give us a "reality check" so that He can reveal to us what's really going on around us and in us.

He will reveal our purpose in life.

CHAPTER 2

The Danger Zone

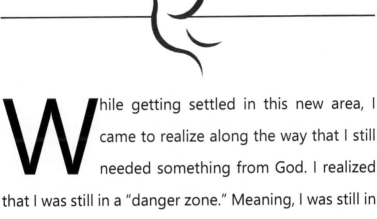

While getting settled in this new area, I came to realize along the way that I still needed something from God. I realized that I was still in a "danger zone." Meaning, I was still in an area of my life of high risk for harm. In other words, I needed salvation and God on my side. I started attending church with one of my family members. As I began to be in the midst of the Word of God every Sunday I began to notice a change in my life.

The more I heard the Gospel the clearer my life became to me. I begin to see and understand truths. You see, God can do anything He wants to do, but with me, I had to walk this out because some things I didn't want to let go of, but God! Let's be real, I was a sinner and a wretch undone and needed to be saved! Even though I cried out to God before, I discovered that it was a cry but I also needed a confession (Romans 10: 9, 10)

I attended church one Sunday and I was so moved by the Spirit of God that I walked to the altar and gave my life to Jesus Christ because I did not want my soul to be lost. I repented of my sin and asked Jesus to come into my heart and save me. God saved my soul from a world of sin and eternal damnation. God saved me and placed my feet on the Solid Rock so that I could stand. Beloved, God can save, deliver, heal, and set you free! I am a witness.

When I gave my life to Jesus Christ, my life changed for the better. Now, I must walk in what God has done for me. I still needed to be sanctified and filled with the Holy Spirit. The enemy still wanted to hold me captive to the things of the world. I started dating and got into a situation that almost cost me my life. How many of us know that we cannot dance with the devil and try to serve God at the same time! We may try but believe me it will not end well. We cannot serve two masters (Matthew 6: 24). We must make up our minds to serve the Lord and Him only. Once we make this decision the Lord will help us in every area of our lives.

What I thought I had to have or wanted, I really did not need at all. I told God if you get me out of this I promise you that I will wait on You. God delivered me from that situation and I kept my promise to Him. I had to get used to walking and living without things and people who I thought were good for me but they were not good for my life at all.

I had to go back to God and repent for getting involved in an unhealthy situation. We were having a Revival and the Spirit of God overshadowed my entire being. When I came through, I was under the front pew at the church. God filled me with the Holy Spirit and my life completely changed. I was so overwhelmed with the Presence of God that the next day, one of the church mothers called to check on me. I told her, "I am trying to get this off of me." She said, " No honey, let

Him stay there as long as He wants to. He is blessing you." I was enjoying the Presence of the Lord.

After that night, I was empowered with the Holy Ghost and began to speak with other tongues as the Spirit of God gave utterance (Acts 2:4). From that day forward, God began to speak to my heart and I was able to understand Him with clarity. God is a Mighty Deliverer! He can and will deliver you from sins' grip. There is no one more powerful than Almighty God. God delivered me and I kept my promise.

CHAPTER 3

No More Damaged Goods

As I look back over my life, there were times when I thought that I would never be good enough for anything. The enemy will have you believing that you are "damaged goods". When a person is considered as "damaged goods", they are flawed or spoiled in character, efficiency, or worth. For example, when UPS delivers your package and it arrives broken or shattered, it is considered as damaged goods. Life experiences can leave us broken and shattered. We all have faced times in our lives when we were devastated, shocked, stunned, and crushed because of hurt, pain, disappointment, abuse, and rejection.

The enemy of our soul comes to steal, kill, and destroy all that God has purposed and destined for our lives (John 10:10), but God has given us life more abundantly. Many of us have thought that we weren't beautiful enough, we weren't great enough, or not smart enough, but I am here to tell you that you are beautiful enough, you are great enough, you are smart enough, and you are good enough! "God saw everything that He had made, and behold, it was very good" (Genesis 1:31). We can no longer allow the enemy of our soul to rob us of our identity when we know that God, the Creator of Heaven and Earth, knew what He was doing when He created us. Many have been through some very hard and dark experiences in life, some have come out, some are still there, and some are no longer with us.

When you have experienced physical and emotional abuse in life, it is very difficult to have a healthy self-esteem or a clear understanding of whom God says you are and whom He has created you to be. People who have never been violated in this way do not fully understand the devastation of the ungodly behavior of others nor how detrimental it could be to one's whole entire being. It is detrimental to the mind, body, and soul. Abuse of any kind causes unwanted, unhealthy behaviors and attitudes. Abuse damages the very being of a person and distorts their true identity and character. The Lord draws near to us when we are broken and crushed in our spirit (Psalms 34:18).

This Earth is full of people with broken hearts, broken spirits, and broken relationships. And we know that broken things are always detestable or considered as being useless. Broken things and broken people in this world are the results of sin.

I am so thankful and grateful that Jesus was wounded and bruised for our iniquities and transgressions (Isaiah 53: 5). Jesus bore our pain, hurt, suffering, rejection, and everything that has caused us not to live a prosperous life. He was wounded for our physical, emotional, and spiritual healing. Jesus' suffering was not for patch-up healing but for complete healing of our mind, body, and soul.

Remember, when we accept Jesus Christ into our hearts as our Lord and Savior, we are no longer "damaged goods." He has healed us and made us complete in Him. Decree and declare every single day, God made me and He did an awesome job! I am good enough and I am more than enough because God said I am His workmanship (Ephesians 2:10).

CHAPTER 4
Fixed Perception

The mind has a way of going in its own way and we have to be very careful in which way it is being directed or being steered. Have you ever heard "Where the mind goes, the man follows," we have found this to be true. For example, when you get up in the morning and you say to yourself "I am going to the grocery store" and then you end up at the grocery store. The mind is not an organ. The brain is a physical organ. The mind is the thought process of reason. It is where thought, imagination, emotions, memory, perception, and determination takes place. The brain can be physically touched but only God can touch and teach the mind. Having the mind of Christ is an awesome and priceless possession (Philippians 2:5).

Human beings have a mechanism known as dualism which views the mind and body as separate actions. Can the mind exist without the body? It is possible because the mind is different from the body. The subconscious mind is a powerful 95% of our brain power and handles everything the body needs to function properly.

Our bodies can change reality. For example, the body responds to stress of any kind. It responds to constant worry, stress over jobs, finances, and other problems that can cause tense muscle pains, headaches, and stomach problems. This can lead to high blood pressure and serious health problems. In order to change the way we think, a transformation has to take place in the mind. Our minds have to be renewed by the Word of God (Romans 12:2). The intelligence of the mind penetrates every cell in our body. The mind has tremendous power. The mind is considered a pure, vibrating energy. Our perception forms our reality. Perception helps us see ourselves, others, and the world. Perception is incredibly subjective. When we perceive something, it means that we identify with the means of the senses. What we feel around us is always evolving. It changes our actions with others and the things around us. Many people have "fixed perceptions."

A "fixed perception" can cause many issues because when something is fixed it's restricted, locked in, settled, and not capable of being rearranged. A "fixed perception" clouds and blurs reality. Sometimes things are not what they appear to be and then there are other times when things are just what they are. Our thoughts have to be governed at all times by the Holy Spirit. By allowing the Holy Spirit to lead us and guide us into all truths, we cannot go wrong. Every day we should choose to make single adjustments in our own thoughts and behavior. When we do this, we begin to see ourselves and our bodies in a whole new life. Allowing God to unfix our perception will help us to see and perceive as He does. It's fascinating and amazing when we look through the eyes of God and see as He sees.

CHAPTER 5

Pile-up "Syndrome"

W hile journeying through life, we can get overwhelmed by situations, problems, and circumstances. If we are not careful, we could end up having a situation I like to call the "pile-up syndrome." The "pile-up syndrome" is when we allow situations, problems, and circumstances to pile up on us in our minds, bodies, and spirit without releasing any of them. When we allow this to happen, we become stressed, heavy, burdened, and pressed down. We should cast all our cares upon the Lord (1 Peter 5:7). Whenever we are going through this, we should take all our cares to the Lord. God knows how to fix every problem in our lives. The more we hold onto it, the more complicated things will get because in this life we will always have to deal with something.

For example, you may be having financial difficulties or just found out that you need another car. Or maybe you just received knowledge that your loved one is sick. This is the beginning of the" pile-up "syndrome". We should choose our battles and then pray about them. There will always be challenges, but we can overcome them if we will talk to the Lord about everything, no matter how small or big the situation may seem to be. After all, small things can pile up and become bigger things.

The world does not stop turning because we have problems or a bad day. The Earth takes 24 hours to rotate once about its axis which equals one day and then the Earth revolves around the sun 365 days which makes one year. It is set in motion by God and this is a continuous process that will not stop for no one. The quicker we give our problems, situations, and circumstances to God in prayer, the better our lives will be. Life is like jumping hurdles and if we don't jump them in a timely manner, the hurdles will eventually beat us down.

We must learn to bring all of our struggles and troubles and lay them at the feet of Jesus. Jesus tells us to come to Him, all of us who labor and are heavily laden, He will give us rest (Matthew 11:28). Always remember that you are not alone and that there's someone else here on planet Earth that has been through what you may be up against. There are others among you who had survived and overcome this very thing that you are going through. Be encouraged and don't get bound up in this web called the "pile-up syndrome."

CHAPTER 6

No More Toxicity

Life has a way of getting us involved in many relationships. It could be marriage, dating, friendship, family, jobs, or business partnerships, and we may not realize that we are in a toxic relationship. What is considered a "toxic relationship?" It means that in the relationship one of the individuals is toxic, or both of the individuals are toxic. Anything that is "toxic" is poisonous, harmful, and unpleasant. A toxic individual is a person who is negative and always brings turmoil to your life. Individuals who are considered toxic are dealing with their own demons of hurt, pain, stress, disappointment, trauma, insecurity, and rejection. You can spot a toxic person when you constantly have to walk on eggshells around them and they displace negative behavior.

Toxic people are always full of drama! Yes, do yourself a favor and get away from them in a hurry! These individuals will poison your character, dreams, goals, influence, successes, and even your testimony of salvation. We must come out from among them and be separate (2 Corinthians 6:17). Signs of toxic behavior include a lack of support, chronic stress, controlling behavior, dishonesty, fear, degrading, stonewalling, diminished self-worth, manipulation, separation from family and friends, and anxiety. Toxicity is like poison, it will destroy and kill you!

Humanly speaking, oftentimes we think that we can do something to help the individual but if that person is not willing to correct their toxic behavior, they will not change. The majority of the time in relationships, you will have one person that would have a willingness to stay predicated on false hope and a potential change but this person is putting their faith in change that would never happen. The only way a person can permanently change is that they must be willing to change. Some people came into this world fighting because the odds were already stacked against them. For instance, raised in a single-parent home, in poverty, surrounded by violence, drug addiction, and abuse. Many people were raised by individuals who were already bruised, battered, and beaten emotionally, spiritually, physically, and mentally. The Bible clearly states, that we were born in sin (Psalms 51:5). We had to fight the devil at the very moment of conception!

The Good News is, there is healing for the soul. God is a Deliverer! The truth of the matter is a toxic person has been hurt or violated in some capacity in life. Therefore, hurt people, hurt people! We must allow God to heal, deliver, and set us free from all our past hurts and pains. If we continue to walk around as if these things do not exist in us, then we are deceiving ourselves and we will not be able to help others. There is healing for the brokenhearted (Psalms 147:3). It is Almighty God who is more than able to perform this.

He is Jehovah Rapha the "Lord who heals thee." Jesus wants us to be made whole.

When we allow ourselves to continually be in a toxic relationship of any kind that says something about our character. We may feel like we are not strong enough to walk away. Also, it could be an underlying factor that allows us to keep accepting this kind of behavior. Whatever the case may be, we must ask God to help us to walk away from such behavior otherwise we become a partaker of their toxicity. We must ask God to cleanse, wash, and purge us from all impurities of the flesh and spirit (2 Corinthians 7:1). No matter where or whom the toxicity is coming from, we must purpose in our hearts and decree and declare there shall be "no more toxicity!"

Promise yourself that you will no longer waste another precious breath or moment on toxicity. When you do, you will be glad that you did. The Fruit of the Spirit will be in operation and there will be no room for toxicity. Love will flow, peace will flow, and joy will flow from your life. Today, purpose in your heart that from this day forward, there will be no more toxicity but productivity, capability, and creativity in your life. God is in the healing business.

CHAPTER 7

Dirty Laundry

We are currently living in a world full of hardships and pain. Especially when people get satisfaction out of airing out other people's "dirty laundry!" Some people get satisfaction in airing out other people's dirty laundry. We must remember that there is such a law as reaping and sowing (Galatians 6:7). If we don't want to reap it, then don't sow it! It is just like the law of physics, " What goes up must come down." When I was a little girl the elderly used to say, "Sweep around your own front door or mind your own business!" In other words, take care of your home and your business and leave everybody else alone. We should practice studying to be quiet and do our own business (1 Thessalonians

4:11). We should not be interfering in matters that do not concern us. It's simple, stop meddling in other people's business and stop being nosey.

Make it a priority to guard your own heart. Be careful and do not be a partaker of "demonic drama!" Believers should avoid quarrels and foul language. Revealing unkind and damaging personal secrets causes division (1 Cor. 11:18). We just jump and do all kinds of stuff. God's children should not argue or discuss unpleasant private things about others in front of other people causing them to be embarrassed. We should not be involved in any ungodly conversations. Let us practice letting our words please and glorify our Redeemer (Psalms 19:14).

When we wash our own dirty clothes or linens, we do not wash them in public. We wash them in the washing machine, with the lid on, to keep them in the washer while they are spinning. And we all know, that when dirty laundry has been washed and cleaned it smells good and fresh! In life, some things should remain personal and private. Remember, we all have to wash our dirty laundry from time to time and if we do not want people to air out our "dirty laundry" then please don't air out no one else personal or private matters. Learn how to pray, say less, and make it our business to keep our minds stayed on the Lord 24/7 (Isaiah 26:3).

Love thy neighbor as thyself (Matthew 22: 39). Meaning, if you want others to respect you, respect others. If you want others to treat you right then you should treat them right. Stop gossiping and start Gospelling! This is better for everyone. And if we have the desire to air out something, let us air out "Jesus saves and God loves you!"

CHAPTER 8

Comparison: The Death Authenticity

Growing up, I always compared myself to other people and it spilled over into my adult life. Over time, I have learned and accepted to be who God has created me to be. When I saw a glimpse of whom God has created me to be, I vowed to praise Him because I am fearfully and wonderfully made (Psalm 139:14). Many of us have compared ourselves to someone else at one time or another in life. When we compare ourselves to others we miss God Almighty, we miss out on all the goodness and authenticity that He has placed within us.

Often times we may see something awesome in the life of another individual but we should not try to be like them. We should allow God to reveal to us who we really are and what He has invested within us to do great exploits (Daniel 11:32b). We were individually crafted and woven by the hands of Almighty God. The Ruler of the Universe, the One who put the sun, moon, planets, and galaxies in motion and still they remain this way even until this very day.

We must learn to cherish and appreciate our own talents, gifts, and strengths. Comparison is the representation of one thing a person is similar to or like another. If there is something that you dislike about yourself, just enhance it without changing your true self. For example, if you don't like the way you dress, hire a stylist to help you. If you don't like your current weight, get a physical trainer. If you don't like your job, find what you would like to do. We have to make the necessary adjustments. We must learn to be happy with who God has created us to be. If not, we will find ourselves being jealous or envious of someone else's life.

A while ago, the Lord gave me a dream and in this dream, there were two individuals that were in a field looking up into the sky. As I proceeded to walk towards them, I looked up to see what they were looking at. When I looked up, I saw an angel holding a beautiful shining, glistening ornament. I stood there with them and we stood there together waiting and anticipating for the angel to release and drop the ornament. These two individuals that were standing there became impatient and walked away. I believe that they got tired of waiting. As they were walking away, I stood in the same place where we were standing before and the angel dropped the shiny ornament, which landed right in front of me, approximately two feet away. I looked at the ornament and as it hit the ground, it began to smoke and sizzle. I walked over to the ornament. I didn't touch it because it was still smoking and sizzling so I waited for it to cool off to touch it. When I picked it up, it was a beautiful ornament.

As I stood there I asked the Lord, "What is this?" He gently replied, "This is a gift". I questioned the Lord about the gift falling only when they left. In a still small voice, God said, "It didn't belong to them, it belongs to you." What I want us to understand is this, what is for you is for you! No one can take anything from you that God has ordained, purposed, and destined for your life." Never compare yourself with another individual because we are all authentic in some way or another. So embrace your authenticity! Refrain from comparing yourself to others because what God has invested in you is just as valuable and important as what He has invested in others. Comparison is the death of authenticity.

CHAPTER 9

Discovering Your Microscopic Self

When we say something is microscopic, we are saying that the object is so small that it is not visible to the natural eyes, not even to those with 20/20 vision. For example, naturally, even with 20/20 vision, we cannot see things like bacteria, viruses, chromosomes, dust, or cells of the body. We would need a microscope to see these small particles. The smallest thing a human eye can see with the natural eye or 20/20 vision unaided by a microscope is about 0.1 millimeters in diameter. For example, human hair.

In order to see the microscopic, we need special tools like telescopes, microscopes, and magnifying glasses. We must understand that God can see past the microscopic view of all His creation. This means that He knows everything about us from the inside out. There is nothing that we can hide from Him because He is omniscient. Meaning, God has "unlimited knowledge". He sees and knows all things. Whatever is microscopic to us is magnified to God. The eyes of the Lord are in every place beholding the evil and the good (Proverbs 15:3).

There are approximately seven billion people here on Earth and no one else has your fingerprints or retina scan. We have our own individual blueprint already created and established by God. We have our own original design. When we take the time to pray and seek God's will, we will discover that we are powerful beyond measure. The closer we get to God, the more things that we did not see in our lives become magnified. The Presence of the Lord has a way of revealing the unseen. God reveals Himself and reveals to us who we really are in Him. We are made in the image and likeness of God Almighty (Genesis 1:26).

God has created you to be a masterpiece. You are unique and authentic and there is none like you, this is Good News! God is the One who controlled our framework at the time of conception while we were in our mother's womb. Psalms 139, pictures God as a "knitter" and we know that those who knit are very precise when they are knitting their masterpiece. He controls the process of our making. It is an honor to be the apple of God's eye (Deuteronomy 32:10). We are God's divine creation. Everything about us has been predestined before the foundation of the world. We were created to be a passionate delight, a considerable honor, with regards to being distinctive and unlike others in a noteworthy way.

We are like rubies rare, expensive, and costly! Discovering who we are on this glorious planet, will cause our self-worth to go up ten notches. We all have gifts, talents, and strengths to help make planet Earth a better place for all mankind. We encourage you to search deep down inside that microscopic part of you, allow God to be magnified in your life, and then you will discover that you are a vessel full of treasure (2 Corinthians 4:7). These treasures are waiting to be revealed in a timely manner. So go ahead and discover you, the one who was crafted and fashioned by the hands of the Creator of Heaven and Earth.

CHAPTER 10

Imperfect to Perfection

The truth of the matter is we are imperfect beings striving for perfection every day. When something is imperfect it is flawed or incomplete. In other words, it needs some work for it to become complete. As Believers when we are striving for perfection we are holding ourselves to a higher standard of living and that standard is holiness. According to James 1:4, It is written that ye may be perfect and complete. God knows that we are not perfect but He wants us to strive for perfection every single day. We are imperfect human beings loving our perfect God. God is perfect there are no flaws, defects, errors, or faults in Him at all.

When we truly, sincerely love God we will desire to please Him in everything that we do. God loves us and His mercy endureth forever. God knows that we will fall short of His glory from time to time in this life. He will always be there to pick us up, strengthen us and give us directions to keep moving forward. God promises to instruct us and teach us the way we should go, He promises to counsel us with His eye upon us (Psalm 32:8). God knows the way that we take. He wants us to follow His instructions and guidance. We strive for perfection by laying aside every weight, spending time in prayer with the Lord, reading and meditating on the Word of God, and having fellowship with the Saints of God.

We must live free from perfectionism. When we are striving for perfection we should be free of fear and anxiety. We must understand that it is God who perfects us (Philippians 1:6). It is God who leads us and guides us. It is God who has saved us, delivered us, healed us, sanctified us, set us free, and filled us with His precious Holy Spirit. As we live for, serve, and love

God Almighty, who is perfect in all His ways and in all that He does, we become perfect day by day. The more we submit to God and walk in obedience the more we become more like Him. We are not perfect but we love God and He loves us regardless of our imperfections and flaws. God is love (1 John 4: 8).

CHAPTER 11

Dungeons and Dragons

I recall a time that I went through a life-changing experience. The spirit of fear had gripped my heart and I started having anxiety problems. I felt like I was walking through a dark, dungeon-like tunnel for two years. I had a dream before this happened. In this dream, I was walking through an open field, and in the midst of this field, I spotted a barn. As I proceeded towards the barn, two older women came to meet me. They were dressed in long, white dresses and both of them had white turbans on their heads. One of them got on my left side, while the other got on my right side. We proceeded to walk towards the barn. Once we approached the barn and opened the door, there were snakes on both sides of the barn. Snakes everywhere!

The snakes were all different sizes, colors, and skin patterns. The two women put their arms under my arms, as to undergird me, and led me through the barn of snakes. Once we approached the back door of the barn, both of the women let go of my arms, went through the door, and left me standing alone. I was so terrified and frightened because I knew what we had just walked through. I called out to see where they were, but there was no answer. I turned around to see if I could go through the back door, but it was sealed and locked from the other side. So at this point, I realized that I had to go back the same way that I came into the barn.

I collected my thoughts and emotions and started calling on the name of Jesus! As I proceeded to walk back through the barn, I saw something that baffled me. All of the snakes that we had just walked through, were dead! They were all chopped up as if a huge lawnmower had come through. Neither one of us had any kind of tools as we walked through the barn of snakes. As I proceeded to go back the way we had come in, I had to walk through ALL THOSE DEAD SNAKES. When I awakened, I prayed and asked God for interpretation. Later on that day, the Lord revealed to me that I was going to have to walk through a very dark and dangerous place and there would be venomous vipers that would be coming against me. God assured me that He would be with me every step of the way (Isaiah 41:10).

Well, it was not long after that dream that I had to face one of the hardest decisions in my Christian walk, divorce. Yes, divorce. Divorce is a heartbreaking, heart-wrenching experience. This is something that I do not wish on anyone but it happens every day and yes, it happens in the Church too. Life is full of surprises but God knew that this was going to happen. I would have never thought in my sweet dreams that this would happen to me in the Church. I was thinking not me, not so but yes it was me and it was so. Again, I will not rewrite the book because what happened made me who I am today. I am more loving, caring, kind, and merciful. Before this happened, I was walking and operating in the spirit of pride and we know that God hates pride (Proverb 8:13).

I had a habit of saying, "I wonder why this and I wonder why that?" But when it came to my front door I was able to understand, "Why this and why that." From that day to this day, I refrained from wondering "why" so much. The reason being when I ask too many questions and I wonder why, I found myself going through that very same thing that I am questioning and wondering about. So now I just pray and seek the face of God.

This experience taught me a lot. It taught me not to be so high and lifted up and to always have empathy toward other people's situation. I always keep in my mind that it could be me! We should never think that things will not happen to us. When we see others going facing any difficult or painful circumstances we should pray and seek the Lord on their behalf. We must understand that we are living in a fallen world and nobody is exempt from calamity or tribulation.

Divorce did not break me but it made me! It gave me a chance and an opportunity to love me and to love who God has created me to be. My aftermath of this situation became a "kairos moment." I began to unearthed treasures within that I have no idea existed. And even though I had to start all over again, I don't regret a thing. In the process of starting over again, the Lord demoted my flesh and promoted me in the Spirit!

Remember, when God has allowed something to take place in our lives, it is not to destroy us but to build us up. It is His way of saying to us that "the voice of the flesh must be mortified" (Romans 8:13). So go through the dungeons, fight the dragons, and destroy the snakes because we always win in Christ Jesus.

CHAPTER 12

Sin's Deadly Hook

S in has an evil bait called "temptation." What is temptation? Temptation is a deep yearning to do something or to have something. Temptation has a negative connotation and is associated with harmful objects and behaviors that have long-term results. Temptations can be overpowering cravings. It is being tempted to do what you should not be doing if you want positive results from something. For instance, eating sweets while dieting, on social media instead of finishing homework, or buying materials things that we cannot afford. Believers are to watch out for being lured toward sinful, risky behavior and ungodly stuff in order to pull us away from God.

Mankind is drawn in a direction of enticement because of his or her own lust (James 1:14). The scripture tells us that temptation comes when we are drawn away by the world and the enemy. When the enemy is providing enticement, it's just like a fish enticed by a bait and then the fish is drawn in. The bait lures the fish into the trap or net. Satan tempts us from day to day and what we must understand is that the only reason why the temptation is able to get its hook in us, is because we are in the flesh and have a fallen nature. Have you ever heard of "delayed gratification?" It means good things come after a prolonged wait.

Most of us have a problem with waiting. Waiting is not for the weak or fragile. The word "wait" is a small word but has its difficulties and struggles in our lives. In order to wait, it requires discipline, patience, humility, and faith. The flesh does not want to wait, it wants everything now. When we wait on the directions and instructions of the Holy Spirit we cannot go wrong. As children of the Highest God, we must follow the leading of the Holy Spirit so we will not get caught up in sin's deadly hook.

Sin pollutes, damages, and sifts the image of God out of your life. There are many baits that the enemy use in the fallen world. These baits are misleading traps. The bait of lust, adultery, pride, jealousy, envy, hatred, gluttony, slothfulness, and the list goes on and on. It is our responsibility to never fall into these traps. When God is speaking to our hearts about any kind of unholy, unrighteous, and ungodly actions, practices, or behaviors, it behooves us to take heed of what God is saying to us. He is trying to warn us of these deadly hooks! Beware of the tricks, wiles, lies, and devices of the enemy. God has given us power over the enemy (Luke 10:19).

If we do not take heed then we find ourselves between a rock and a hard place and it will take God to intervene and pull us out of the snare of the enemy (Psalms 124: 6-8). Do not get entangled with this world's way of thinking and doing. We must be sober-minded and watching because the enemy is always seeking to destroy someone's life and testimony. Believers should be submitted to God at all times so that we can resist the devil and he will flee from us (James 4:7). We have continual victory in Jesus Christ!

CHAPTER 13

The Invisible War

Have you ever been going through something and couldn't quite understand what it was? Have you ever felt an uneasy presence that seems to follow you everywhere you go or be present in almost everything you do? You cannot seem to put your hand on it or even recognize what it is that's making you feel uneasy. Well, my friend, this is what we call an "invisible war!" We are in an ongoing battle with evil forces and we may not always know initially what we are battling against, but one thing is for certain we know that it is an evil force. This is why we must make sure that our spiritual armor is secured and in place in order to fight against the wiles of the devil (Ephesians 6:11).

We cannot see this "invisible war" with our natural eyesight. This war is spiritual and must be fought in the spiritual realm. We cannot fight an "invisible war" with carnal weapons. Our weapons cannot be fleshly, they must be spiritual to break and destroy yokes and pull down strongholds (2 Corinthians 10:5).

The spiritual realm is impossible to see with the naked eye. It is hidden, covered, concealed, masked, veiled, undetected, mysterious, and undercover. To some, this war is invisible but to others it's visible. There is always a war going on between good and evil because the flesh is constantly warring against the Spirit, and the Spirit against the flesh. We know that a war is a conflict between groups or different groups. In this case, God Almighty and His army of angelic beings are at war against all demonic forces. There is a continual spiritual war going on in the heavens.

This is a true story. I was going through something and what I was going through was very unfamiliar. This situation puzzled me. I prayed and meditated on the Word of God but it seemed as though this unholy, ungodly, illegal presence would follow me everywhere I went. One day in prayer during 50 days of fasting and praying, the Lord spoke to me and said, "Sever the head of the boa constrictor!" I was blown away because the Lord has never spoken to me in this way. I asked the Lord. "What do you mean "sever the head of the boa constrictor?" At this point, I'm saying to myself, "What, a boa constrictor?" Now, I am aware that I'm fighting against an evil, vicious demonic force.

I went to a dear friend of mine, a Servant of the Lord. God's servant would pray for me and prayer would strengthen me but the war did not cease. God's Servant said to me, "You have to stand up to the devil!" I was crying, shaking, and terrified because I have never had to stand up to this kind of evil force. I said, "I don't know how to stand up to this right here." Either I was going to stand up or be devoured and defeated by this evilness. I was not about to be devoured and sure did not want to be defeated. I begin to seek the Lord for direction, wisdom, and instructions. Let me tell you something, God showed me how to stand up against that evil force that was attacking and tormenting me. I started exercising and executing my God-given authority over that evil force and the evil attacks ceased.

Dearly Beloved, the spiritual world is real! The enemy was bold and he showed me exactly who he was and what he was doing. He was torturing and tormenting me! I was saved and there was no known sin in my life that I was aware of. I repented and repented again. I thought that I had done something wrong and this is why this was happening to me.

The Lord reminded me that He had given me power and authority over all the works of the devil. From that day forward, I begin to stand in the power and the authority that God had given unto me. God said, Behold, I give unto you power tread on serpents and scorpions, and over all the power of the enemy: and nothing shall by any means hurt you (Luke 10:19). When I began to take authority over the spirit of the boa constrictor, I was delivered and set free by the Power of the Blood of Jesus, the Word of God, and by the Power of the Holy Ghost! Hallelujah, to God be all the Glory!

Believe it or not, there is always disunity, collision, vendetta, feud, discord, encounter, and bad blood between the flesh and the Spirit. Therefore we fight in the Spirit against principalities, powers, rulers of darkness, and spiritual sickness in high places (Ephesians 6:12). We always win and conquer in the Spirit realm. Therefore we must not neglect prayer, fasting according to the will of God, reading, and meditating on the Word of God. This is how we maintain the victory in Christ Jesus against every "invisible war." God will bring all things to light. He will reveal to us who we are fighting against. Ask God to open your eyes so that you may see what it is that you need to see. In order for us to maintain total victory in our lives, we must have spiritual eyesight and insight. God has given us what we need to conquer every "invisible war!"

CHAPTER 14

Life Glassiness

Be careful of being transparent! It is all right to be transparent just make sure that the Spirit of God is leading you to reveal your transparency. We must always remember that the spirit of jealousy is waiting on our transparency or our glassiness. There are people that are in our midst that is waiting and anticipating something that is supposed to help others or to shed some positive light for good, but instead, they want to get it, run with it, and assassinate your character with it. We must understand and know that there are individuals who want to see us fail. They want our relationships, goals, marriages, careers, and everything that will cause us to be prosperous, to come tumbling down. Be careful! Sometimes your friend is not your friend, sometimes your ace is not your ace! Most of the time, these individuals become your greatest enemies or greatest critics.

God sees and knows all. There is nothing hidden from God. If the truth be told everyone lives in a glass house when it comes down to God Almighty because He knows all things. He is omniscient. We cannot hide anything from God! He knows our uprising and our downsitting (Psalm 139:2). He knows what we are thinking, how we are feeling, what we want to say, and so on.

I always tell people to tell God the truth. He already knows. He already knows if you are angry, fed up, had enough, or just done with it! Jesus has already gone through what we are going through. He was tempted in all points, but He did not sin (Hebrews 4:15). We know that glass is breakable, and at high pressure and force can be shattered. Glass when broken or shattered can never be restored to its original state.

We can glue the pieces back together but there will always be a piece or pieces missing. We can melt it back down but there will still be some glass missing. Our lives are just like glass they can be broken and shattered by the things that we go through in this life. Sometimes, we are broken and shattered and we need God to put the broken pieces back together again. And the piece or pieces that are missing are supposed to be missing. It is God's way of separating us from things and people that we no longer benefit from our purpose in life and there should not be no love lost.

God is the only one that makes a shattered and broken life whole again. He is a skilled expert at everything He does. God can and will save, deliver, heal, and make us whole again! He can make us over again! He makes all things new. There comes a time in our Christian journey when we will experience some brokenness for the glory of God. If there is no suffering then there is no reigning with Him (2 Timothy 2:12). Natural glass when broken is damaged and will never appear the same way again, but The Potter is able to take a broken, shattered, and messed up life and put all pieces back together again. We will not even look like what we have been through! So be transparent but always be led by the Spirit of God when you are revealing your transparent moments to other people. And remember, our lives are just like glass to God and there are no secrets to Him. He looks down from Heaven and sees everything crystal clear. Amen

CHAPTER 15
The Secret Chamber

We have had many experiences with God. There was a time when I was going through a difficult situation. I felt down all the time, nothing seemed right, worried, frustrated, and all the above. I went before God in prayer. I believed if I could just get in the Presence of the Lord that He would reveal to me what was really going on. I was right! He revealed unto me that what I was going through and that thing that I could not see was "melancholy." I said "Melancholy!" I recall hearing this word from somewhere and I knew it had something to do with depression. I continued to pray and to thank God for revealing to me what I was battling with. God will never leave us in the dark because He is light and in Him, there is no darkness at all (1 John 1:5). I Googled the word "melancholy" and as you know we can Google anything! The word "melancholy" is defined as a feeling of sadness with no obvious cause. It means a sad, gloomy, and mild depression. God revealed to me what was really going on and taught me how to pray against the spirit of melancholy (mild depression).

Yes, I was fearful. Fear gripped my heart because during this time I was also in spiritual warfare dealing with another situation. I was reminded of the Word of God that teaches us not to fear and that we have power, love, and a sound mind (2 Timothy 1:7). Can I be real? It felt and seemed like I had been placed on the doorstep of hell! I was scared because I never had to fight on this level before.

Spending time in the secret chamber helps us to get better acquainted with our God and ourselves. It's a beautiful thing to go into the secret chamber with God and come out with joy, peace, healing, deliverance, an answer, a solution, strategy, strength, or enlightenment. Our God is an awesome God! We must make it our priority to always visit our secret chamber daily so that we can know and do the will of God. According to scripture, in the Presence of the Lord, we can experience the fullness of joy (Psalms 16:11).

There are many places on earth that we may call our secret chamber but in this case, we are talking about the throne of God. We have the invitation to come boldly to the throne of grace, obtain mercy, and find grace in whatever we need (Hebrews 4:16). A secret chamber is a private room where you may go to conduct meetings and personal affairs. These rooms are places that are secretive and nobody knows what's going on inside except the people that are involved. Believers' secret chambers are known as the prayer closet and only God and the Believer know what goes on in the prayer closet. God knows everything. He is omniscient. This is the place where we can be honest, open, and transparent with God and ourselves. We can tell him all about our troubles, struggles, challenges, and problems. We have been awarded an awesome divine privilege that we can take everything to God Almighty in prayer.

God reveals Himself to us in the secret chamber. He will also reveal to us who we are and where we are falling short as well. God loves us so much that He even reveals to us what we really mean to Him. There is no better place to be than in the secret chamber with God Almighty. In there, we find refuge and strength, joy and peace, mercy and grace, and goodness and lovingkindness! When we are there, we are under the shadow of the Almighty (Psalm 91:1), dwelling in His safety. So we encourage you to make it a priority to dwell, bask, and abide in your secret chamber with the Lord daily.

CHAPTER 16
Considered By God

Have you ever asked God "Why?" Why are these things happening? What have I done so wrong? or Why me? When we are faced with difficult times, being "considered by God" is the last thing on our minds. We are just trying to figure out how to get through this or how to get out of this! In my life, I have asked God many questions about why this happened or why that happened. Today, some of those questions have been answered and other questions have not been answered at this time. Even though some questions have not been answered, God has given me peace in the midst of these unanswered questions.

I still believe that on this Christian journey, God will answer questions that need an answer in this life. In the Bible, Job was one of the most upright and perfect men in the Old Testament. Job was considered by God (Job 1:8). Job went through many things. He lost his children and his wealth. His wife even said to Job, "Curse God and die" (Job 2:9). But through it all, Job held on to his integrity. Oftentimes, we go through things in this life and some of us have had somewhat of a Job Experience but God! I questioned God many times when I was growing up because I did not understand the things that had transpired in my life. I was bullied in school because my classmates didn't understand the struggles and challenges that I was facing from day to day during this time. I was retained in the 7th and 8th grades, not because I didn't do my work or my lessons, I was retained because I did not have a mind to go to school. My teachers knew that I had potential but I could not see it back then. They knew that I was a smart, intelligent young lady but I had some challenges. When I look back and I think about this time of my life I know God was with me all the time.

I was able to pass the 7th grade and 8th grade. I was an alternate cheerleader in the 6th grade. An alternate cheerleader was the person who would take the place of another cheerleader who was absent. The Lord blessed me to graduate from the 8th grade to the 9th grade. In high school, I played junior varsity basketball. I was a point guard because of my height. After a season of basketball, I lost interest in extracurricular activities at school and began to hang out in places that were not good for me. I didn't have anything else to do concerning school besides schoolwork. How many of you know that if you don't put some on your mind the devil will? My high school experience would be an interesting one. I began to party and hang out late and had to be at school the next morning. I would get up to go to school and be hanging over from partying all night. One particular morning, I was so embarrassed because I looked like I had been out all night and some of my classmates were giving me the side eye, but they never said a word. At this time, I really did not have any guidance and for those who really cared about my situation, I did not have an ear to hear what they were saying. I was just trying to find my way and that was the only thing that I knew to do. The Lord blessed me to go through high school and to be honored to receive a "Lieutenant Governor's Award" for writing a paper. This was very encouraging to me because in this I saw some of my potential.

I had no intention to go to the prom or to do things that other young people desired to do during this time in my life. While my classmates were buying prom dresses and getting beautiful for the prom, I was getting ready to go to the club. In the midst of it all, God blessed me to be able to finish high school and receive my high school diploma in 1989. I'm thankful and grateful because I needed that diploma because God knew that I would continue my education in the near future.

During my high school years, I also had my own apartment and another great responsibility. I had bills to pay, make sure food was on the table, and make sure that everything that comes with a household responsibility was taken care of. There were times that I felt that life was unfair and that I had been dealt some unwanted and unnecessary cards. I was eighteen years old and at this age, I should have been living my best life. but God brought me through. I have no regrets. I am again grateful and thankful because, all of this, made me a better person.

Today, I want to see young people get educated and be successful in this life. I speak highly of education because I believe that education has awarded me to finish high school and obtain an Early Childhood Diploma, Nursing License, Master in Divinity Degree, CPR Coach Certification, wrote my first book "The Fabulous Life of Quincina Davis", and many other awards and achievements. I give God Almighty all the honor and the glory for the things He has done in my life (Jeremiah 29:11). My greatest achievement of all was when I accepted Jesus Christ as my Lord and Savior! So when I look back over my life and see all the things that I have been through I can truly say that I'm grateful and I'm thankful that I was considered by God. No, I didn't have a Job Experience but I had a God Experience.

There were people that were looking for my downfall but they didn't know that I was "considered by God!" Some said that I would never amount to anything or that I would never be anything but God had my life in His hands. When you have been "considered by God", He has already planned your future, we just have to make the decision to follow His directions. So I will say unto you, no matter how hard it gets, no matter what it looks like, what it feels like, or what it seems like, remember God has considered you and He will bring you through everything that you may encounter in this life. We all have "why's" and we may not get an answer to all of the "why's" but God! He will give us the strength to keep pushing and moving forward. So rejoice, knowing that it is truly a blessing to be "considered by God". What a Mighty God we serve!

CHAPTER 17
My Spiritual Navigator

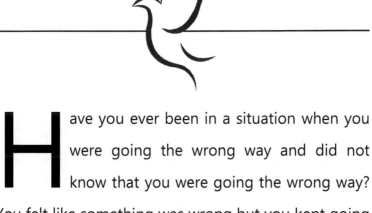

Have you ever been in a situation when you were going the wrong way and did not know that you were going the wrong way? You felt like something was wrong but you kept going in spite of what you felt tugging at your heart. You knew within yourself that you did not have a clear vision of moving forward but you proceeded anyway! Well, when we reach this point in our journey we definitely need our "navigator", the Holy Spirit. We need Him to map out the route we should take.

Today we use and rely on Global Positioning System (GPS). It is computerized equipment that is designed to take us anywhere in the world. Just like the GPS has the capacity to direct us where to go worldwide, the Holy Spirit directs us and instructs us on which way to go and what paths to take. It is vital that we humble ourselves and obey His voice.

The Holy Spirit is the greatest navigator we will ever need. He leads and guides us into all truths (John 16:13). A navigator is responsible for directions and decides on what course of action to take. This individual provides us with understanding and helps us to be aware of any obstacles, barriers, or hindrances. The Holy Spirit does not leave you confused. He makes things clear and understandable. If for any reason you have clouded judgment or debatable guidance, pray again and again if necessary, because God is not the author of confusion (1 Corinthians 14:33).

The Holy Spirit gives us the accurate and correct information to follow. The natural navigator of a ship has to be accurate in their instructions otherwise, they run into some unexpected trouble and become shipwreck. There should not be any struggle or conflict when the Holy Spirit is leading you. He knows where to go because He has already been where we are going. I don't know about you but I would rather follow someone that has already been there than someone who has not. I would prefer following someone to a different city or state that they have been to before, it would make me feel somewhat comfortable following them because they have traveled these roads before.

As a navigator, the Holy Spirit will give us wisdom and knowledge. Also, He may lead us to our spiritual fathers, mothers, leaders, or counselor for instructions and directions. He makes righteous and just movements. We must trust Him to lead and guide us in all of our decision-making. He truly is a lamp unto our feet and a light unto our path. We need light to see which way to go. It is not wise to make decisions in the dark because we cannot see the whole picture. My navigator is the Holy Spirit. He is my helper, comforter, and teacher (John 14:26).

An important fact to remember is, the Holy Spirit never does anything except what is written in the Scripture. Our navigator the Holy Spirit has the ability to lead us in our walk with the Lord, in our marriages, in our relationships, and in whatever decision we have to make along this journey. Allow Him to be your navigator because when we follow Him we cannot go wrong.

CHAPTER 18
Finding Quincina

As I sit here and think about my life, I have been blessed. God has blessed my entire life. I thank God for my past, present, and future. The Lord has helped me to accomplish many extraordinary things. He has blessed me to raise and teach two amazing children as a single mother. I know what I want, what I don't want, what I refuse to put up with, and what I desire in this life. I am so grateful and thankful that I have had the privilege of finding myself for the last 10+ years. God has been an amazing counselor, navigator, comforter, and teacher in my life. Thank God for my Lord and Savior Jesus Christ and the precious Holy Spirit that leads me and guides me into all truth.

This time of finding me has been a great adventure and I know that I will discover more about who God has created me to be. In the pursuit of finding me, I discovered that I had a lot of unresolved hurt and pain. God had me walk out all of it so I can tell you what pain feels like. I can tell you what rejection feels like. I can tell you what depression feels like. I can describe to you what fear feels like. I can tell you what anger feels like. I can tell you what a violation feels like. I can tell you what loneliness, shame, sadness, disappointment, humiliation, abandonment, and brokenness feels like. And the list goes on and on!

But the most amazing thing about this is, I can also tell you what agape love feels like. I can tell what peace feels like. I can tell you what joy feels like. I can tell you what freedom and liberty feel like. I can tell you what grace, mercy, hope, gratitude, thankfulness, compassion, empathy, confidence, beauty, happiness, and comfort feels like! I can definitely tell you and describe to you what satisfaction feels like because right now with breath in my body, I can truly say that I am so satisfied with my Lord and Savior, Jesus Christ!

I am not perfect nor will I ever be perfect but I strive for perfection every day and I know that I have a testimony. Life situations and circumstances have not been easy but I have a testimony. When I think of all of the things God brought me through and where he brought me from, I have come to the conclusion that there is nothing worth me losing my relationship with God for or losing my soul for! Absolutely nothing! My covenant with God Almighty means more to me than anything in this whole world. God has blessed me with more than I ever had in my life. I took full responsibility for my actions and for any offense towards anyone. I was not perfect neither was I the bad guy or the evil one. I refuse to accept anything less than what God has for me. I am forever and eternally grateful for all of the things that God has done for me. It is up from here and I will not accept anything less. I want a little Heaven here on Earth. This is not pride, it is being secure and sure that whatever work God has started in us, He is more than able to execute or carry it out until it is completed (Philippians 1:6). He still working on me as I am yet in pursuit of discovering my entire purpose. What a wonderful, marvelous, extraordinary adventure it is when you discover your God-given purpose here on Earth! This is a great and rewarding mission to accomplish.

CHAPTER 19

Forgive And Live

n order to forgive, you must be willing to forgive. If we are honest and sincere we all have had a situation or circumstance in our lives when we had to forgive someone at one time or another. If you have not had to forgive someone, eventually you will because it is inevitable. Before we can forgive, we need to know about unforgiveness and what it means not to forgive others. Unforgiveness is an emotional or cognitive distress that results in delaying a response to forgive someone that has offended you. Unforgiveness is poisonous. It will erode your character and integrity. When an individual is walking in unforgiveness he or she is walking in resentment, anger, rage, and even wrath. An unforgiving person is a dangerous person because the majority of the time they seek revenge.

An unforgiving person wants you to be punished and pay for what you may have done to them. Unforgiveness causes us to relive what the offender did to us. We keep rehearsing it over and over in our minds. We keep talking about it with our family, our friends, our coworkers, and just sometimes anyone who will listen. A person who chooses not to forgive harbors resentment in their heart, and God is not pleased with this. The Bible states that if I regard iniquity in my heart, the Lord would not hear me (Psalms 66:18).

Unforgiveness hinders our prayers, our relationship with God, and our connection to Him. In order to forgive, we must be willing to let go of the offense and the offender of the offense. We must release all things to God. We have to ask ourselves, do we want to be free from the offense, do we still want to be angry and resentful about it or do we want to keep heading down this course of demolition? The choice is ours. I have had a situation where I had to forgive more than one individual of an offense, through and by the grace of God I was able to forgive.

Some offenses are deeper than others. This depends on the person and nature of the offense but we must forgive them all. When we choose to forgive, God will heal us! God healed me from the pain, the hurt, the humiliation, the guilt, and the memory of many offenses and violations.. You see when God heals, He heals! He does not leave a residue! When it's done, it's done! Jesus bore all of our pain, grief, and sorrow on the cross so that we could experience divine healing, salvation, peace, and joy (Isaiah 53:5). After I repented and received my healing I was able to witness the Goodness of the Lord to the one that offended and violated me. Remember, no one can forgive another individual for you. Walking in unforgiveness will stagnant your growth in God and forfeit your blessings. We must make the choice to forgive with the help of our Heavenly Father. When we forgive, we begin to live our best life and the life that God Almighty has promised to us. We walk in joy, peace, freedom, and love. It is God's desire that we live without regrets, offense, worry, or guilt. We must learn how to forgive and live. Forgiveness is good for the soul, so forgive and live.

CHAPTER 20

My Spiritual Life Jacket

Imagine one day you and your friend are at the swimming pool. Your friend is swimming, then all of a sudden she gets a cramp in her leg and can no longer swim. She is crying out for help, so the lifeguard jumps into the pool and rescues her to keep her from drowning. As the lifeguard is on his way to rescue her, she is floating on top of the water waiting on the lifeguard. What keeps her from drowning and sinking? A life jacket. What if she didn't have on a life jacket? Would she have survived? Probably not. I thank God for our spiritual life jacket called faith. The lifeguard saw that she had not given up or thrown in the towel. She was waiting in faith for the lifeguard, who would come to rescue her. This was an earthy lifeguard but Jesus

Christ the Son of the Living God is our Spiritual Lifeguard. He came to rescue us from permanent death and condemnation.

We must always wear our spiritual life jackets, that is our faith, confidence, and belief in our Lord and Savior Jesus Christ. What is a natural life jacket? It is a personal floating device to save a life in water. It helps us to stay afloat and prevents us from drowning. In the natural, swimmers wear life jackets to keep them afloat if something goes wrong while swimming. It keeps the swimmer from drowning and keeps the swimmer in an upright position in order to keep the mouth and nostrils free of water. The swimmer waits patiently for the first responders to rescue them.

We encounter situations that come and almost drown us. Some of the waves and currents in life throw us for a loop. We need to faithfully keep the faith because we have no idea when the next wave of problems and trials is going to hit our lives. Exercising our faith is a good practice from day to day so that we will be equipped to weather the storms of life. When the pressures of life are caving in on us God wants us to have faith in Him (Mark 11:22), knowing that He has everything under control. Consistently wearing our spiritual life jackets and having faith to believe God, will bring great rewards. When we come to God we must believe He is God and that He is a rewarder of those who diligently seek Him (Hebrews 11:6).

Continue to wear your spiritual life jacket at all times. Don't take it off or put it down for anything. We need it to keep us afloat and alive. We always need, now faith! Now faith is the reality of hoping for something, that shall be clearly seen or understood in the future (Hebrews 11:1).

CHAPTER 21

The Golden Rain

Gold is one of the most precious and attractive elements on earth. It is attractive because of its brightness and splendor! Gold is recognized as one of the most concentrated of all metals. It has been studied and found to be an excellent doctor for heat and electricity. It is a highly favored, pleasing, workable, and durable material. According to the Periodic Table, Atomic Number 79 is the element for gold. Gold's symbol is Au. Gold was the first and oldest form of money (Genesis 2:12). Gold is recognized as the currency of queens and kings. Gold allows access to all locks. No latch, bolt, or chain will grip the influence or control of this element.

During a season in my life, I was going through a period of lack and drought. I was feeling like everyone was being blessed except for me. I was doing all I knew how to do to serve God and yet I still felt like God had forgotten all about me. How many of us know that that is not true? God will never forget about us. One thing is for sure He will never leave, abandon, or give up on us (Hebrews 13:5).

God gave me another dream to encourage my heart. In the dream, I was sitting in the choir stand, and as the minister began to preach all of a sudden this little girl walked up to the choir stand. The minister turned around and said to the little girl, "Go and touch the person to whomever the Lord leads you to in the choir stand". The little girl started walking in the front row. She began to stretch out her hand to touch another individual on the front row but then immediately she drew back her hand. As she proceeded to walk down the front row, she looked at me and smiled. She grabbed my hand and proceeded to lead me off of the choir stand, through the side door, and into the parking lot.

While she was leading me out of the church building, she never said a word. When we arrived outside in the parking lot, she instructed me to raise both of my hands up in front of me in a cuplike position. I lifted my hands up in a cuplike position and it started raining. I began to fasten my eyes on the rain. I began to notice that this was a different kind of rain and that it was not ordinary rain. It was the most glorious rain I have ever seen. I was fascinated by all of the beauty of its brilliance. As it continues to rain, I did not see the little girl anymore. She led me into the rain and left me there! As I stood there in the rain, I looked down at the palms of my hands and I saw something glistening. I looked again and I saw small pieces of gold falling into my hands. It was raining and the rain had gold in it! I was standing there getting drenched and soaked in golden rain. This is my "Golden Rain" Experience!

Gold represents riches, splendor, authority, wealth, and security in the spiritual realm. God promised to bring us to a "wealthy place" (Psalms 66:12). God has a way of encouraging our hearts. God gave me the strength to do what He knew I was capable of doing. He gave me favor and put the right people, in the right place, at the right time. He knows what we need, and He will meet us at that need anywhere, anytime, and any place. Remember, God is there whenever we need Him. Allow Him to rain on your life and reign in your life.

CHAPTER 22
Heaven is Calling

H eaven is a real place. It is not this magical place some may not think exist. Heaven is the place where God's people will live for eternity. It is a place of peace, harmony, and goodness. Heaven is a prepared place for a prepared people. It is a place of wonder, glory, and splendor. It is God's dwelling place. Heaven is a place where the streets are paved with gold, the walls are made up of beautiful jewels, and every gate is one pearl.

The voice that we hear, the crowd of words and sentences that are penetrating from up above the heavens is the Calling of Heaven! There was a young child by the name of Samuel in 1 Samuel Chapter 3. This young man had been set apart for the work of the

Lord at a very young age. In 1 Samuel Chapter 3, Samuel was in the temple with Eli the priest one night and Samuel heard a voice. This voice spoke and said "Samuel." Samuel ran into the room of Eli the priest but Eli did not call Samuel's name. Samuel heard the voice calling his name again, and then the third time. Eli stated once again I am not calling you but the next time you hear this voice say, "Speak Lord for thy servant heareth" (1 Samuel 3:10). God was calling Samuel. Samuel was a prophet of Israel.

Some of you may have heard the Lord calling you by your name. When He called you by your name, did you answer him? Or did you ignore the voice of God? Bible teaches us, that if we hear His voice hardened not our hearts (Hebrews 3:15). In this life, we face many challenges. Many times, God uses trials, tests, illness, calamities, or even tragedy in order to get our attention. Have you ever experienced something called consecutive test traps? Consecutive test traps are when it seems as though the tests would never end! We must understand that God is trying to get us to listen to Him. God is always calling us to another level in Him. Heaven is calling!

Yes, we may have brought some things on ourselves but even in the midst of it all, God still loves us. He will be right there even when we fall short of His glory (Romans 3:23). We have a loving. caring God that will never give up on us even when we still choose to disobey Him, We must continue to be diligent in keeping our eyes, ears, and hearts open to the call of Heaven. Heaven is calling!

When we call He will answer us and while we are yet speaking, He will hear us (Isaiah 65:24). In the year 2004, I was attending an initial sermon service of a young lady who had accepted the call of God. I will never forget that night. She preached from Luke 4:18. I received the Word of God that night and the Presence of the Lord was upon my life that night like never before. After the service was over, I went out of the side door because something unusual was happening to me and I did not understand what it was. As I was driving home, the Presence of the Lord was in my car so strong that I wept all the way home. God begin to deal with me about preaching His Word. At first, I did not know what to do because this was new to me and all I wanted to do was to live holy.

How many of you know that God does not take "no" for an answer? I tried to suppress what was going on in my spirit but I could not. Finally, I told God yes! This is not the first call. The first call was the call to salvation into the Body of Christ. I am so thankful and grateful that I took heed to the voice of God! It is a privilege and honor to be called by Heaven. Many are called but few are chosen (Matthew 22:14). When Heaven is calling you and you are God's choice, not man's choice.

Let us learn how to embrace and accept the fact that God has chosen us to be His ambassadors and representatives on Earth. Get ready! God has chosen us and given us divine favor from the foundation of the world (Ephesians 1: 4-6). Heaven is calling!

CHAPTER 23

Heaven is Coming

We believe that angels exist and are still among us. Angels are God's messengers. They come on the scene with a specific purpose. They are divine helpers who bring divine assistance, enabling power, and strength. When we get in trouble and need God's help, Heaven is coming! I am reminded of Daniel's prayer (Daniel 10:12) when he prayed and did not get a response from the Lord for twenty-one days. God heard Daniel when he prayed but the answer to his prayer was opposed by the prince of the kingdom of Persia. Then God sent Micheal the Archangel to help expedite the answer to Daniel's prayer. God answered his prayer. No matter what kind of situation we may face in this life, when we are going through a situation God will send comfort, hope, protection, and direction, and divine assistance.

God sends his messengers to bring a message from Him. We all need divine help from time to time. When Daniel was in the lion's den the Lord sent an angel once again and shut the lion's mouth (Daniel 6:22). God loves His children and will move Heaven and Earth for them.

Have you ever had a difficult moment or season on this Christian journey? Well, if you have not, just keep living because this is a tedious journey. I recall a time when I was having a difficult time and God spoke through one of his servants about sending me divine assistance. This divine help was two angels that were dispatched to protect me and my household. A couple of weeks after it was spoken to me, I saw in a vision two big creatures with wings descend from a cloud. As I got closer and took another look I saw that it was two angels. They were watching over me and my household as the Servant of the Lord had spoken to me. When I saw those two angels I knew that everything was going to be all right because God had sent me divine assistance (Psalms 91:11).

God genuinely loves us and cares about us. He cares about the great things and the small things. Whenever we are in trouble and need divine assistance God will send Heaven to come and assist us with whatever we need. When God hears His sons and daughters crying in pain and distress, discombobulated, and fearful, He is moved with compassion and His next move is to come on the scene to fix what is broken up in us. That which is broken up in you and that which is broken up in me, it does not matter to God where it came from or who did it, He is there to fix what is broken! Be encouraged and have faith in God because when the righteous cry, Heaven is Coming!

CHAPTER 24

Smile, You Are on Heaven's Camera

One day, while I was taking pictures I looked up into the sky and it dawned on me that Heaven has a camera too. What, Heaven has a camera? Yes, but not the camera that we use here on Earth. Heaven's camera is the eyes of the Almighty God who sees all, knows all, and hears all. God is sitting on the throne watching everything we do, whether we believe it or not. The Lord sees everything and everybody, all of the good and the bad (Proverbs 15:3). This lets us know that we cannot hide anything from Almighty God.

Therefore we must be mindful of what we do and say because Heaven has eyes and ears.

There was a popular television show back in the day, this show would tell you to smile and they would take a picture of you doing the most or God knows what. This show would capture secret films of people and they would use them to make people laugh but the person on the camera was being humiliated. More like today, when people prank you or film your mess ups and bloopers. They film your most embarrassing moments and moments that make you look indecent. It's sad today that some people find other people's public embarrassment and humiliation funny. Sometimes without permission, we are on a camera that we had no idea was rolling. We are living in a time when individuals will post everything negative instead of posting everything positive on social media. Nowadays, some people will get a good kick out of making others feel embarrassed. Some people think that it is okay to embarrass and humiliate people for a good laugh but if the shoe was on the other foot, they wouldn't feel that way if someone did that to them.

Let's talk about a natural camera. A natural camera has many parts but we're going to talk about two of those parts: the aperture and the image sensor. The aperture is the opening in front of the camera. The most significant section of the camera is the image sensor. It is known as the heart of the camera. This part decides the image or resolution. In other words, what the image would look like or its outcome. The aperture is like the door to Heaven or the opening of Heaven. The image sensor is the image that God sees when he looks at His Creation. It is what God sees when he looks at you and I. God sees us as His chosen generation, a royal priesthood, a holy nation, and a peculiar people (1 Peter 2:9). When God looks at us He wants to see Himself and if he does not see Himself, then He puts us back on the potter's wheel (Jeremiah 18: 1-4). One thing about me is that I like taking pictures. I like to take them for memories. There was a time when I didn't like taking pictures. The reason was, the picture that was being taken did not look good enough for me. The person who took the picture did not catch my best side so I would move to avoid being seen in any pictures or any pictures that were taken. We know that in God when He looks down through His heavenly lens of His heavenly camera we cannot hide. There is no ducking and dodging in God. He sees everything. He knows everything. He hears everything. We cannot hide from God Almighty.

There are approximately 7 billion people here on Earth and there are numerous places and spaces. God is so awesomely powerful that He can see all of us, hear what we are all saying, and see what we are all doing, and where we are at the same time. Our God is an awesome God. So the next time we decide to take a selfie or any other picture let this resonate in our mind and remember that Heaven has a camera too. Be careful how you live, how you walk, how you talk, how you present yourself, and how you treat other people. Remember God is watching. Smile, you are on Heaven's Camera!

CHAPTER 25

The King is Coming

We have been told for many years that Jesus is coming back. Well, it is true, He is coming back! As Believers, we live so that we will see this great day. In 2001, I wanted to become more knowledgeable about the Word of God and my Lord and Savior Jesus Christ so I started attending Bible College. I wanted to know what I had to do, in other words, what kind of life was required of me to go back with Him when He came to rapture His people. My heart was fixed and still is to this present day, on this glorious event that shall take place one day in the future (1 Thessalonians 4:16-17).

During this time, I had a dream. In the dream, I saw Jesus coming! At the beginning of the dream, I was downtown in a large city. Everybody seems to be having a pleasurable time. They were shopping, spending money, and buying whatever they wanted to buy. It was obvious that their minds were fixed on whatever it was that they were doing. I kept getting the unction to look up. As I looked up at the sky, I noticed that the sun was shining so beautifully. It was so bright. All of a sudden, a thick, white, and fluffy cloud appeared in the middle of the sky. While still gazing at the cloud, the wind began to blow in the center of the cloud, it looked like a strong whirlwind. The wind continued to blow and as it was blowing it opened up the cloud from one end to the other end. What I saw next was fascinating, amazing, and intriguing.

In the opening of the cloud where the wind was blowing appeared an angelic host. There were angels from one end of that cloud to the other end. They were hanging and floating in midair. As I continued to look at this amazing site, I saw this huge figure walking

120

towards the angels. This huge, human-formed, figure had wide, broad shoulders that stretched from one end of the sky to the other end of the sky. When I looked closer, I saw Jesus coming in great power and glory! And when I say great power and glory, this is the best description that I can think of but it was so much more! When the Bible speaks that the heavens of the heavens cannot contain Him, I believe it to be true (1 Kings 8: 27).

I was so happy. There was a joy that I have never felt before in my life. I started yelling "Look, Jesus is coming, !" Nobody heard a word that I said. Nobody stopped doing what they were doing. I kept shouting "Jesus is coming!" It seemed like something had been pulled over their ears preventing them from hearing me. Immediately, my joy and excitement turned to disappointment because nobody was listening and the saddest part was that nobody saw Him coming. We should do our very best to keep our lives in order so that we do not miss the Rapture. We should live all we know how to live, pray all we know how to pray, give all we know how to give, and love all we know how to love according to God's divine will and way. Because believe it or not, Jesus is coming!

My prayer is that you were able to gain some knowledge and wisdom to help you in your everyday walk with the Lord. I hope that this book has been a blessing to you and to all that shall read it. I have learned not to take all of my "victories" to the grave but to share them while I am here on Earth so that they will be a blessing, strength, and encouragement to someone else. I encourage you to share your story because you are a survivor to someone at this time who is a victim and they need your story.

May the Lord bless you and keep you,

May the Lord make His face shine on you and His grace

cover you,

May the Lord lift up His countenance on you, and give

you perfect peace. Amen

(Numbers 6: 24-26)

Made in the USA
Columbia, SC
06 May 2024

34989165R00070